THE TREASURES THAT TEACHERS TRADE AWAY TO MAKE OTHERS RICH, YET THEY REMAIN POOR

Maxwell Steindacruz

Book and Cover design by iMax Concepts

CONTENTS

INTRODUCTION

Teaching is a noble profession that involves imparting knowledge and shaping the minds of the next generation. Teachers play a crucial role in shaping society's future, and they are often revered and respected for their contributions. Teachers often begin their journey with a deep sense of idealism. Fresh-faced and full of passion, individuals enter the profession with a burning desire to make a difference in students' lives. They spend years acquiring knowledge, honing their skills, and investing their time and energy in their craft. Their commitment to education is unwavering, driven by a genuine belief that teaching is a noble and rewarding profession. However, after a few years of teaching, they realized that teaching was not a rewarding profession. Their passion for teaching began to fade gradually. They quickly realized that there was a glaring disparity between the amount of wealth they created for school owners and the amount they earned. Teachers struggle to make ends meet despite their immense contributions to society. In this book, we will explore the treasure teachers have trade away to make others millionaires, yet they remain poor. Any teacher who is serious about becoming a millionaire can benefit from reading this book, whether they teach in public or private schools.

CHAPTER 1: THE VALUE OF EDUCATION

Education is often touted as the key to success, and rightly so. It can transform lives and create opportunities once thought impossible. Teachers are at the forefront of this process, imparting knowledge and skills to their students. Yet, despite the critical role teachers play in shaping the next generation, many educators struggle to make ends meet. In "The Treasure that Teachers Trade Away to Make Others Millionaires, Yet They Remain Poor," we delve into the complex and often hidden forces that keep teachers trapped in a cycle of poverty even as they are in the field of opportunities where they can easily become millionaires. The question you and I need to answer is: where does the money generated by teachers go? Why are teachers not well paid? Why are teachers not respected like other professions? And why are so many people leaving teaching for a better job? I would like to state here that the problem teachers in private schools face today started when education was commercialized.

The commercialization of education

In recent years, education has become increasingly commercialized, with private schools charging exorbitant fees. This has created a situation where education is no longer a right but a commodity that is only available to those who can afford it and the profits keeps flowing to administrators, corporations, and investors, rather than those who actually teach. In spite of the high tuition fees charged by these schools, teachers are often underpaid. In the education industry, wealth is transferred to investors rather than teachers. Now that we have delved into the genesis of the problem, let us look at the people who make millions from the education industry. Even as teachers continue to wallow in abject poverty.

The wealth of the education industry

The education industry is a multi-billion-dollar industry, with companies and individuals making vast fortunes from it. From textbook publishers, education-technology startups to e-learning platforms, the education industry has spawned wealthy individuals and corporations. However, the people who create value—the teachers—often struggle to make ends meet because money does not come directly to them but rather to school owners. Teachers often find themselves caught in the crossfire of profit-driven interests that prioritize financial gains over educational quality. Many teachers face the pressure of meeting profit-driven goals rather than focusing on their students' best interests. The tension between commercial interests and educational values leaves teachers conflicted and disheartened.

CHAPTER 2: THE DEMANDS ON TEACHERS

Teaching is a demanding profession that requires time and energy. Teachers often work long hours, spend weekends grading papers, yet they struggle with low salaries, inadequate resources, how to deal with disruptive students, and heavy workloads that leave them exhausted and overwhelmed. Despite these demands, teachers are not compensated adequately for their efforts and are often treated as second-class citizens. In this book, I recognize the incredible dedication, passion, and talent that so many teachers bring to their work every day. I would like to state here that the once-bright passion of teachers fades as they confront the harsh realities of the profession. That is why I challenge teachers with the secrets in this book to be intentional about becoming millionaires so that society can honor and value them like other noble professions because of the crucial role they play in our society. Now let's look at the other challenges teachers face on a daily basis.

Note: Thick (YES/NO) if any of these apply to you, and rate yourself on a scale of 100. Rating the challenges you face daily will allow you to be more intentional, which will help you leave the rat race and become a millionaire.

Everyday challenges teachers face

It is imperative to note here that education challenges

are complex and interrelated. Many teachers confront these challenges daily. Teachers face overcrowded classrooms, lack of resources, outdated curricula, and bureaucratic and administrative burdens. The emotional toll of the job is another challenge that teachers struggle with. These challenges include the pressure of meeting performance metrics and the impact of societal issues such as poverty and trauma from students. With all of these challenges that teachers face in shaping the future of our society, it is sad that teachers are not getting the support and motivation they deserve to succeed in the teaching profession. The following are everyday challenges faced by teachers.

The paradox of teacher training: Does this apply to you? (YES/NO)

Teachers undergo rigorous education and training to become qualified professionals. Traditional teachers are trained through preparation programs to face the harsh reality of obtaining degrees and certifications. In addition, they face the challenges of navigating the complex landscape of professional development. After securing a job, a teacher faces the problem of the mismatch between theoretical training and the realities of the classroom. In addition, there is a lack of support for new teachers and a disconnect between academia and practice.

Challenges of accessing professional development: Does this apply to you? (YES/NO)

In order to effectively meet the evolving needs of students and the requirements of a modern education landscape, teachers require ongoing professional development. Many teachers face barriers to accessing these high-quality professional development opportunities, such as time constraints, lack of funding, or limited resources. It cannot be overstated how important continuous professional development is for teachers; educators must also receive training. However, there is not enough or no support for their ongoing growth and professional development.

The lack of support: Does this apply to you? (YES/NO)

Teaching is a labor of love that comes with personal sacrifice. Teachers often lack support from the government and wider society. They are not given the resources they need to do their job properly; many teachers provide extra support to their students; some use their own money to purchase classroom supplies; and some sacrifice their personal time and well-being to meet the demand. They are often blamed for the failings of the education system. This lack of support makes it even harder for teachers to create value and make a decent living.

The textbook trap: Does this apply to you? (YES/NO)

Textbooks, once seen as essential tools for teaching, have become a costly burden for both teachers and students. Textbook publishers have a stranglehold on the market, charging exorbitant prices for revised editions that are updated frequently, rendering older versions obsolete. Teachers are often forced to use outdated or inadequate textbooks due to budget constraints. This limits their ability to provide the most up-to-date and relevant learning materials for their students. As a result, teachers must find creative ways to supplement their instruction, often at their own expense.

The cost of living: Does this apply to you? (YES/NO)

The cost of living is increasing all over the world, and teachers are not exempt from this trend. Housing, healthcare, and other essential items have risen significantly in recent years. Teachers, who struggle to make ends meet, find it even more challenging to survive in such an environment.

The emotional toll of teaching: Does this apply to you? (YES/NO)

In order to pursue their passion for education, teachers sacrifice many things. Teachers often face the challenges of achieving work-life balance and maintaining a fulfilling personal life while being dedicated educators. Teaching is not just physically demanding but also mentally taxing. Teachers often deal with high levels of stress, burnout, and mental health challenges due to the pressures of the job. This includes the emotional labor of supporting students who may be dealing with trauma, mental health issues, or other challenges such as strained family relationships. There is a need for greater support, self-care, and recognition of teachers' emotional labor. But sadly, the caregiver is not well cared for in our society, and there is no compensation for teachers' efforts in building and shaping the next generation.

Low pay for teachers: Does this apply to you? (YES/NO)

Teaching is often seen as a low-paying and low-status profession in many societies. People from higher socio-economic backgrounds may be more likely to choose professions seen as more prestigious or financially rewarding. Over the years, teachers have been systematically underpaid. The persistent issue of low pay for educators, despite their critical role in shaping the future generation, is very bad; many teachers struggle to make a livable wage. Teacher salaries often lag behind those of other professions, even with similar levels of education and experience. The disparity in salaries can lead to financial stress, forcing teachers to do multiple jobs, take loans from banks, or struggle to make ends meet. Teachers' low pay has negatively impacted their quality of life. There are several factors that contribute to why teachers are paid relatively low salaries compared to other professions. Below are some of the factors that contribute to teachers' poor salaries.

Factors that contribute to teachers' poor salaries

Underfunded education systems: In many countries, education budgets are limited, leading to inadequate resources and underfunding of teachers' salaries.

Lack of political priority: Education is not always a top priority for governments, and as a result, teacher salaries may not receive the same level of funding and attention as other public services.

Economic conditions: In some areas, the local economy may not support high salaries for teachers. This is particularly true in rural or economically depressed areas.

Social status: Teaching has traditionally been viewed as a "caring" profession, and as such, it may not carry the same prestige or earning potential as other fields.

Gender bias: Historically, teaching has been dominated by women, and research has shown that professions with a high proportion of women are typically underpaid.

It's worth noting here that reasons for low teachers' salaries can vary widely depending on the specific country, region, and context. However, it's clear that providing adequate compensation and support for teachers is critical to attracting and retaining talented educators who can help build strong and effective education systems.

Note: What percentage do you have?
Remember: Rating the challenges you face daily will allow you to be more intentional, which will help you leave the rat race and become a millionaire.

CHAPTER 3: THE IMPORTANCE OF TEACHERS' LEADERSHIP ROLE IN OUR SOCIETY

Despite these challenges, teachers remain a vital part of society. They shape the minds of the next generation, and their efforts have a lasting impact on the world. Teachers are not just classroom practitioners but also leaders in their schools, communities, and the broader education system. Teacher leadership has enormous power and a positive impact on student outcomes, societal advancement, and policy change. Teachers are instructional coaches, mentors, and caregivers, to name a few. Teachers shape our society and future generations. On a daily basis, teachers put a lot of effort into their craft; they use their time, energy, creativity, problem-solving skills, and expertise to make others better people because they are selfless leaders. But sadly, society does not recognize teachers' efforts at their craft. Society views teachers' selfless leadership roles as a labor of love, which is why teachers must reposition their image to reach the pinnacle of their careers.

Repositioning teachers' image and reimagining the profession

Education is the key to a better future, and teachers unlock that potential. This book explores all possibilities for repositioning the teacher's image in society and reimagining the future of the teaching profession in order to elevate teachers' status. This includes exploring innovative models of education that prioritize the well-being of students and teachers, reevaluating the role of standardized testing and commercial interests in education, advocating for fair and competitive salaries for teachers, and recognizing the immense value of teachers as professionals and leaders in the field of education. This book calls for collective action and systemic change to ensure that teachers are respected, supported, and empowered. This will enable them to fulfill their vital role in shaping the next generation. As the book goes further to reveal the secrets that can make teachers millionaires, it leaves readers with a sense of urgency and a call to action, urging them to recognize the treasure of knowledge, dedication, and passion that teachers bring to their work and to join the movement to ensure that teachers are no longer trading away those treasures for the benefit of others alone. It challenges readers to use these treasures to better their lives and become changed people. As a result, they will be able to reimaging the teaching profession's future in a way that will honor and elevate it as it rightfully should.

What if I told you that despite all of these challenges faced by teachers daily, there is a way to escape this dilemma? You can become a millionaire. The secret is in this book and I will show you how you have made others millionaires and yet you remain poor; it is time to take the bull by the horn.

Is financial gain part of your motivation: Does this apply to you? (YES/NO)

Have you ever heard people say that becoming rich is not the primary objective of teachers or educators? While a teaching career can be rewarding in many ways, financial gain is also part of educators' motivation. The reason for this is that teachers and other professionals go to the same market and teachers are also entitled to a decent salary. Teaching is a profession that requires dedication, diligent work, and commitment. Many teachers prioritize making a positive impact on their students' lives over accumulating wealth. Teachers find fulfillment in their work by seeing their students grow, learn, and succeed, and by contributing to their community's development. Of course, teachers need to earn a decent living, and it is paramount to compensate them fairly for their work. However, many teachers argue that their worth transcends beyond their paycheck. Many teachers or educators want to own a school so that money comes directly to them. However, owning a school requires a lot of capital and resources. Many people from affluent backgrounds may have the financial means and connections to start and operate a private school or invest in education ventures. Furthermore, it is imperative to note that not all wealthy individuals choose to invest in education. We must commend the people who invest in education. It is also worth mentioning that there are many people from diverse backgrounds who pursue careers in education. These careers include administration, school counseling, educational research, and other roles in the education sector. Career choices are influenced by a wide range of factors, including personal interests, values, opportunities, and resources. They also need to be compensated for their efforts in educating the future generation.

Factors that influence career choices in education

There are many reasons why many people pursue teaching as a profession. Why did you pursue teaching as a profession? The following are reasons why many people choose teaching as a career. If your reason matches mine, choose one. There are several motivations that drive individuals to enter the field, their passion for shaping young minds, and the idealistic vision of making a positive impact on society through education, the joy of witnessing students' growth and success, and the deep sense of purpose that fuels teachers' commitment to their craft. Let's delve into the noble aspirations that draw many to the teaching profession.

Passion for education: Does this apply to you? (YES/NO)

Many people become teachers because they have a strong passion for education and want to make a positive difference in the lives of their students.

Love for working with children: Does this apply to you? (YES/NO) Teaching is a great career for people who enjoy working with children and young adults.

Job security: Does this apply to you? (YES/NO) Teaching is considered a stable profession with good job security, as teachers will always be needed.

Fulfilling and rewarding work: Does this apply to you? YES/NO)

Many teachers find the work fulfilling and rewarding, as they have the opportunity to shape future generations.

Summer breaks: Does this apply to you? (YES/NO)

Teachers often enjoy summers off, which allows them time to travel, spend time with family, or pursue personal interests.

Ability to make an impact: Does this apply to you? (YES/NO) Teachers have the ability to make a positive impact on their students' lives, helping them succeed academically and personally.

Flexibility: Does this apply to you? (YES/NO)

Teaching can offer flexibility in terms of schedule and location, as many teachers can work part-time or from home.

Income and financial resources: Does this apply to you? (YES/NO) Individuals from lower income families may have fewer financial resources to pursue higher education and professional development opportunities. They may also have to work part-time or full-time jobs to support themselves, which

can make them to pursue advanced degrees or certifications in teaching.

Social networks: Does this apply to you? (YES/NO)
People who come from families with social networks that include teachers, school administrators, or other education professionals may have greater access to information about teaching as a career option, as well as opportunities for mentorship and guidance.

Access to quality education: Does this apply to you? (YES/NO) Individuals who attend high-quality schools may have better academic preparation and more confidence in teaching as a career. Conversely, those who attend lower-quality schools may have less confidence in their academic abilities and be less likely to pursue teaching as a career.

Lack of comprehensive career guidance: Does this apply to you? (YES/NO) Lack of adequate information about various career options can indeed influence some individuals to choose teaching as a career path. When individuals are unsure about the opportunities available to them or are not adequately informed about different professions, they may gravitate towards more familiar options or those that seem accessible. Teaching is a field that many people know due to *their own experience in schools and with teachers*. Without comprehensive guidance or exposure to diverse career choices, teaching can appear as a reliable and fulfilling option.

Lack of opportunities to secure a good job: Does this apply to you?(YES/NO) Securing a good job can indeed influence individuals to choose teaching as a career. When the job market is competitive, and suitable employment options are limited, people may consider teaching as a stable and accessible profession. Teaching often provides a relatively secure employment outlook, especially in high-demand subjects or areas where qualified educators are scarce. This can make teaching an attractive option for individuals who struggle to find other job opportunities or worry about job security.

CHAPTER 4: PERCEIVED STATUS OF THE TEACHING PROFESSION

Is the teaching profession worth sacrificing time and energy for? Before I reveal the treasures you can use personally to make yourself rich and become a millionaire, I want to emphasize that sacrificing your time, energy, expertise, creativity, and problem-solving skills will not make you rich but only make you part of the survival race. These efforts only contribute little to making you a millionaire. In history, no one who exchanged time and energy to work for others became a millionaire. Make sure you read this book to the letter so that you can understand what you need to do to become a self-made millionaire teacher.

Perceived status of the teaching profession: How do students, parents, and society perceive the status of their teachers? Have you heard of this before? (YES/NO)

What you are about to read in this book is a true-life story of how students and parents perceived the teaching profession. What I am sharing in this book came as a result of an argument that arose between two teachers and some students during a career day. As you know, Career Day is an event typically held in schools where professionals from various fields are invited to share their experiences. This is done to provide insight into different careers. This year's Career Day saw students choose a career and wear a costume to represent the profession on the day. During school, students can pick a career. Their parents receive a consent letter that encourages or allows them to do so. This will help students make informed decisions about their future ambitions. Many students choose Engineering, Medicine, law, etc., but no one wants to become a teacher. Even teachers' children don't want to become teachers. Only one child chose teaching as a profession before work closed that day. However, when that child returned the consent letter the following morning, the story changed. The parent changed the child's career to law, so the teacher asked all the students who intended to be teachers. There was no one interested in teacherhood.

The class teacher begins the class by asking, "Who is a teacher?" Students give many answers. One child, however, told the teacher a funny definition of a teacher, saying, "A teacher is a person we can make angry whenever we like." The class became very noisy after his funny definition of what a teacher is. The teacher repeats the question, asking if there is any student who wants to become a teacher. There was silence in class that day. During the class, the teacher asked the students about their perceptions of the teaching profession. These are the endless responses she received from students.

1. Teachers are poor.

2. Teachers are poorly compensated; my parents told me their reward is in heaven.

3. Teachers are under too much pressure, they work around the clock.

4. Teaching is a demanding profession that requires time and energy.

5. Teachers are not given the same respect or recognition as

other professions.

It is worth noting here that there could be several reasons why students might be hesitant to choose a teaching profession during career day. Listed above are some possible reasons why students dislike teaching. However, students' career interests can evolve and change over time.

In the wake of that short debate, a Teaching Assistant (TA) in the class interjected that teachers can also be rich. The students asked the Teaching Assistant (TA) to mention a teacher who became a millionaire. But the Teaching Assistant (TA) was short of words and quickly changed the topic to "who taught doctors, who taught lawyers, who trained engineers". The class answered 'teachers' and the students said teachers are not rich and respected like other professionals in society.

I was standing by the window listening to the conversation between the teachers and the students because it was my turn to take the class. I entered the class and told the students that teaching is a noble profession. I made it clear that everyone is a teacher. I said if you can teach your friend 1+1, you are a teacher. I told the students that a doctor who trains other doctors is a teacher too; teaching can take place outside and inside a class. I taught the topic I was meant to teach that day. But after my class, I started thinking about what the students said about teachers being poor. The subject matter got me thinking, especially when they asked the Teaching Assistant (TA) to mention one rich millionaire teacher. I started researching and googling topics like "A millionaire teacher" and "Is it possible to become a millionaire as a teacher?" but to my dismay, I only found two teachers who developed software and became millionaires. I was surprised to see that, as noble as the teaching profession is, one cannot become a millionaire through it. I continued my research, and I found something interesting in one article: "Money does not come directly to teachers' pockets but to the school owners". The article further states, and I quote, "The education industry is a multi-billion-dollar industry, with companies and individuals making vast fortunes from it." From textbook publishers to educational-technology startups, the education industry has spawned a host of wealthy individuals and corporations. However, the people who create the value—the teachers—often struggle to make ends meet".

As a teacher, I was pleased to find a solution to the problem of why teachers are poor. In spite of this, I continued to wonder why teachers who create value are poor. I continued my research on the missing piece of why teachers are poor. I found many materials that talked about what a teacher could do to become a millionaire. These are the lists of things I found unhelpful, among others.

1. Mindset: You must change your mindset about money. Tell yourself you are a millionaire.

2. You can't trade time for money and become rich.

3. Portfolio diversification: Have multiple sources of income.

3. Risk Taking: A school owner is a risk taker, which is why he or she created the business to hire you, but a teacher is not.

4. Upscale yourself: The degree you have today will become worthless when a child you taught in grade five possesses the same degree.

5. Learn high-income skills.

The results I got were not satisfactory, and I knew something was missing. The teacher taught business entrepreneurs, bankers, lawyers, business owners, and doctors, to mention just a few. But why is the trainer not a millionaire? I started googling and reading books about this topic but found no answer. It's as if nobody knows the answer. During my research, I saw something captivating in one of Steve Harvey's videos: "You cannot google success on the internet." This quote got me thinking for months, but then I realized that I could not find the answer I was looking for on the internet. I have to find it within myself.

I finally found the answer!

This secret I want to show you in this book, "The Treasures That Teachers Trade Away to Make Others Millionaires, Yet They Remain Poor," is a case study of many years of research that nobody has ever shared with any teacher in the past. As a teacher, you will become a millionaire once you understand these points. This book is not like other books that do not explain the main point immediately. Let me go straight to the main point.

The pathway to becoming a millionaire teacher: What I discovered after years of research

Firstly, the type of job you have affects whether you become rich or not. For example, individuals working in the finance industry are better placed to obtain and evaluate information on how to invest and what to invest in. However, teachers do not have access to this information about making millions. The only financial information teachers have access to is what they use in class, home lessons or online tutoring, and selling things, none of which can make them millionaires. The distinction between an individual working in the finance industry and a teacher is the kind of job they do. This puts one at a higher advantage to make more money because of their access to financial information. To get out of this rat race, you must position yourself so that you can get access to information that can change your life. You can do this by attending seminars and workshops in finance and investment.

Before I explain the second point, I would like you to think about this popular quote that says **"Every idea you need to succeed is in someone's head".** It is worth noting here that most of the ideas students used to create big businesses could be traced back to their teacher.

Secondly, the secret is the concept of "Ideas." Thousands of ideas come to light during teaching, and many students quickly use them to create businesses that make them millionaires. You must know how to process and evaluate these ideas efficiently during your lessons. Teachers freely give students ideas, but they don't understand how to use them themselves. Many teachers don't recognize the value and worth of the ideas they trade away. Teachers freely share these ideas with their students. They broaden students' mindsets to create businesses or inventions that change the world. And yet, they don't know the value of what they trade away. Take a minute and think about this question.

"Why are many millionaires school dropouts?" The answer is not far-fetched; it is because they quickly heard the ideas a teacher was trading away without knowing it, and they turned those ideas into big companies that brought in millions of dollars. That is why they dropped out of school to pursue the idea. The question is, do you know how many ideas you have thrown away to make others millionaires? Considering the number of years you have spent teaching, after every lesson, do you always reflect on those traded ideas that can make you millions, or do you just leave them out there for others to become millionaires? One of the mistakes you can make as a teacher is not knowing when ideas come and how to transform them into millions.

The story of students who turn teachers' ideas into wealth:

Now let's look at FedEx's story and some other stories to see how teachers teach others to become millionaires through their ideas. However, teachers cannot use the same information to become rich. **Note:** *The key points are bolded so that you understand where the ideas come from.*

FedEx's revolutionary overnight delivery

FedEx's story is known in business circles. It is a story of perseverance, determination, and innovation. The company was founded in 1971 by Frederick W. Smith, a student at Yale University. While studying at Yale, **Smith was listening to a lecture about the inefficiencies of the transportation industry.** The lecturer argued that the industry was slow, unreliable, and expensive. Smith was struck by this idea and began to think about how he could solve the problem. He envisioned a company that would offer overnight delivery of packages, with a focus on reliability and speed. This idea was revolutionary at the time, as overnight delivery was not yet an established service in the transportation industry.

Smith wrote a paper about his idea for an overnight delivery service as part of a class assignment at Yale. His professor was unimpressed with the **idea**, giving him a C for the paper. But Smith was undeterred. He believed in his idea and knew that it had the potential to change the industry. After graduating from Yale, Smith founded Federal Express (now known as FedEx) with the goal of revolutionizing the transportation industry. He faced many challenges in the early days of the company, including financial difficulties and technical problems. But he persevered, working tirelessly to build a company that offered reliable, speedy delivery services. In the years that followed, FedEx became a major player in the transportation industry. The company's innovative approach to overnight delivery, with its focus on reliability and speed, proved to be a game-changer. Today, FedEx is one of the largest delivery companies in the world, with a global network of operations that spans more than 220 countries and territories.

The story of FedEx is a testament to the power of determination and innovation. Frederick W. Smith's vision, born from a single lecture, has transformed the transportation industry and helped shape the modern world. This story is about how teachers/lecturers always trade away treasures every day because they did not position themselves to process the same information well enough to become millionaires. Thinking is good business, but teachers don't see it from that perspective. They challenge their students daily with different ideas that they should have used to make millions. There are many stories of successful business tycoons who got their ideas from listening to their teachers. I believe that as you read these true-life stories, you will reflect on the past ideas you have traded away to make others millionaires, and now that you are intentional about making millions, you will be conscious of grabbing the next idea that comes your way and creating the next big thing out of it.

Let's look at other **similar stories** of students who got their ideas while **in school** and used them to create **big companies.**

Instagram: Kevin Systrom and Mike Krieger, the co-founders of Instagram, **got the idea for the photo-sharing app while taking a class on mobile programming at Stanford University.** Their idea was inspired by photo-sharing apps on the iPhone, and they decided to create a similar app with simplicity and ease of use in mind.

Groupon: Andrew Mason, the founder of Groupon, **got the idea for the daily deals website while attending an entrepreneurship class at the University of Chicago.** A discussion about collective buying inspired him to create a business that would offer discounts to customers if enough people signed up.

Dell: Michael Dell, the founder of Dell Computers, **got the idea for his business while taking a pre-med class at the University of Texas.** He noticed that students in the class used calculators to do math problems. He realized that there was an opportunity to create an affordable and easy-to-use computer.

Twitter: Jack Dorsey, the co-founder of Twitter, **got the idea for the microblogging platform while taking a course on SMS messaging at New York University.** He was inspired by the idea of sending short, simple messages that could be easily shared with others. He decided to create a platform that allowed people to share short updates with their friends and followers.

Dropbox: Drew Houston, the founder of Dropbox, **got the idea for the cloud-based file storage service while a student at MIT.** He was frustrated with the difficulty of keeping his files in sync across multiple computers. He was inspired to create a solution when he forgot his USB drive at home and had to take a bus back to retrieve it. He developed the first version of Dropbox while attending a lecture in his computer science class at MIT.

PayPal: Max Levchin, the co-founder of PayPal, **got the idea for the online payment system while attending a cryptography class at the University of Illinois.** He was interested in finding a way to make online payments more secure. He came up with the idea of an online payment system that uses encryption to protect users' financial information.

Google: Larry Page and Sergey Brin, the co-founders of Google, **developed the search engine algorithm while working on a research project for their graduate studies at Stanford University.** They were trying to find a way to organize and search through the vast amount of information available on the internet. They developed a complex algorithm that ranks web pages based on their relevance to a user's search query.

Microsoft: Bill Gates and Paul Allen, the co-founders of Microsoft, **got the idea for the software company while working on a computer program for their high school's computer club.** They were inspired by the idea of creating software that would make computers more accessible and easier to use.

Apple: The story of Apple's origins is well known. In the mid-1970s, Steve Jobs and Steve Wozniak attended Homestead High School in California. Jobs was interested in electronics, and Wozniak was a computer whiz. One day, **in a computer design class,** Wozniak showed Jobs a computer he had built. Jobs was impressed and realized that there was a market for personal computers. They founded Apple Computer, which became one of the most successful technology companies in history. As you can see, the amazing idea of selling personal computers came when they were in school. It means the teacher has said something that challenges them.

Some teachers are smart too; they don't trade away their ideas; they keep them to themselves and use them to change the world. These teachers had a passion for education and teaching. However, they also had an entrepreneurial spirit and a desire to create something bigger than themselves. Over time, they began to see the potential for incorporating the ideas they had gained from their teaching experiences to create successful companies and organizations. Below is a list of teachers and lecturers who used their own ideas to build big tech companies.

Teachers turned millionaires through ideas.

The first of these teachers was *Jimmy Wales*, the founder of **Wikipedia**, who got the **idea** for the online encyclopedia while **teaching** a class on internet entrepreneurship at the University of Alabama. Inspired by the thought of creating a collaborative platform where people can share their wealth of knowledge and expertise, he created a platform to connect people and share their expertise.

Salman Khan. Salman had been **teaching math** to his cousins and found that he could explain complex concepts in a way that made them easy to understand. He started creating YouTube videos to help others learn, and eventually founded **Khan Academy**, a non-profit educational website that provides free online courses in various subjects.

Next was *Andrew Ng*, who **taught** computer science at Stanford University. He co-founded **Coursera**, an online learning platform that offers courses and degrees from top universities, after seeing the potential for using technology to make education more accessible and affordable.

Naveen Jain, another **teacher**, was teaching entrepreneurship when he realized that many of his students were struggling with health issues. He founded **Viome**, a company that provides personalized nutrition recommendations based on gut microbiome analysis, to help people improve their health.

Sebastian Thrun taught artificial intelligence at Stanford when he co-founded **Udacity**, an online learning platform that offers courses in technology, business, and data science. He saw the potential for using technology to democratize education and make it accessible to everyone.

Reshma Saujani was **teaching** in New York City when she noticed a gender gap in technology. She founded **Girls Who Code**, a non-profit organization that aims to close the gender gap in technology by teaching girls to code.

Elon Musk, another **teacher**, taught physics at the University of Pennsylvania when he co-founded **PayPal**, an online payment system. He went on to found SpaceX, Tesla Motors, and SolarCity, using the skills he gained as a teacher to revolutionize the tech and transportation industries.

Barbara Oakley taught engineering at Oakland University when she co-founded **Mindshift**, an app that helps users learn new skills and overcome learning challenges. She saw the potential for using technology to help people learn more efficiently and effectively.

Jack Ma, a former English **teacher** in China, founded **Alibaba Group**, a multinational conglomerate specializing in e-commerce, retail, and technology. He saw the potential for using technology to connect businesses and consumers around the world.

Wendy Kopp was **teaching** in a low-income community when she founded **Teach for America**, a non-profit organization that recruits and trains college graduates to teach in low-income communities. She saw the potential for using education to address social inequality and improve the lives of disadvantaged students.

Finally, **_Reed Hastings_**, who **taught** high school math, co-founded **Netflix**, an online streaming platform for movies and TV shows. He saw the potential for using technology to disrupt the traditional entertainment industry and provide consumers with more choice and convenience.

These teachers all had different backgrounds and experiences, but they shared a common passion for education and a desire to make a difference. By using the ideas they gained from their teaching experiences to create successful companies and organizations, they were able to revolutionize industries and change the world for the better.

You are the next teacher who will change the world. Are you ready?

Where and how do I get these ideas?

Several schools and the ministry of education have created avenues to get these ideas, but many teachers are not looking in that direction. They think schools are punishing them with activities like film production, Spelling Bee, Career days, Mental Math competitions, Active learning, etc. Despite all these activities designed to bring out the best in teachers and students, many teachers couldn't come up with one idea that could generate wealth.

Film production, for example, should train teachers to become scriptwriters, costume designers, stagehands, etc.

STEAM (**Science, Technology, Engineering, Art, and Mathematics**) has brought about many remarkable research projects created by teachers, and yet many teachers cannot grab these ideas and transform them into wealth.

Spelling Bee: All you need to do to make a Spelling Bee book a best-seller is come up with a catchy title like "Spelling Bee Pass For Sure."

Active learning: on the other hand, engages students in hands-on experience. During the preparation of the lesson plan, many teachers do a lot of research and improvise, but many do not see ideas that can change their lives in this area.

CHAPTER 5: IDEAS RULE THE WORLD

Becoming a millionaire through the evaluation and processing of your ideas requires knowledge, skills, and a mindset. Here are some steps you can take to achieve your goal:

Develop a renewed mindset: To effectively evaluate and process the ideas that come when you teach, you need to be alert and always ready to grab some ideas during your teaching. This includes knowing how to listen to yourself, identify a promising idea when you present it to others, and re-invent the idea to become a problem-solving service.

Stay up-to-date: Before you can come up with promising ideas, you need to stay up-to-date with the latest news and trends. This can be done by reading news in your area of specialization, reading publications, following relevant social media trends, and attending seminars and conferences.

Analyze the idea: You need to be able to analyze your ideas and propose solutions that can change the world through your ideas. For example, some people believe that trash can be turned into wealth or that waste can be turned into cash. These are ways people analyze the problem they solve and create a brand name through it.

Make informed decisions: Based on the analysis of your ideas, you need to be able to make informed decisions about investments, business opportunities, and other decisions. This requires sound judgment and critical thinking skills.

Manage risk: Successful investors and entrepreneurs know how to manage risk. This means you need to understand the risks associated with different investments and minimize those risks.

Have a long-term focus: Building wealth through ideas always take time, and it requires a long-term focus. You need to have the discipline to stick to your vision, mission, and passion for a long term.

Continuously improve: The teaching world is constantly changing, so it's important to continuously improve your knowledge and skills. This means reading, learning from experts, and seeking out new ways of doing things.

By following these steps, you are on the right track to becoming a millionaire if you evaluate and process your ideas effectively. However, it's important to remember that becoming a millionaire requires hard work, discipline, and a willingness to take calculated risks.

CHAPTER 6: FROM TEACHING IDEAS TO BUILDING COMPANIES

Turning teaching ideas into a million-dollar company requires a systematic approach that involves evaluating and processing these ideas effectively. Here are some steps to turn your teaching ideas into a million-dollar company.

Identify the most promising ideas: Start by collecting all the ideas that come up during your teaching sessions. Evaluate them based on their uniqueness, potential market size, feasibility, and profitability. Focus on ideas with the highest success potential.

Research the market: Once you have identified the most promising ideas, conduct market research to validate them. Look for competitors, potential customers, and market trends that could affect the success of the idea. This will help you refine the idea and identify potential barriers to entry.

Develop a business plan: A business plan is essential for turning an idea into a successful company. It outlines your goals, strategies, and financial projections. Use your research to develop a solid business plan that includes a clear mission, a target market, marketing and sales strategies, and financial projections.

Build a team: Building a team with the right skills and experience is critical to the success of any company. Look for individuals with expertise in areas such as marketing, finance, operations, and product development. Ensure that they share your passion for the idea and are committed to making it a success.

Secure funding: Starting a company requires capital. Consider various funding options, such as venture capital, angel investors, or crowd funding. You can also bootstrap your company by using your savings or taking out loans. Make sure you have enough capital to cover the startup costs and the initial stages of the company's growth.

Launch and iterate: Once you have secured funding, it's time to launch the company. Use your business plan as a guide and execute your strategies. Be open to feedback from customers and investors, and iterate on your product or service based on their suggestions.

In summary, turning ideas that come during teaching into million-dollar companies requires a systematic approach that involves evaluating the ideas, researching the market, developing a business plan, building a team, securing funding, and launching and iterating the company. With persistence, hard work, and a bit of luck, you can turn your idea into a successful company.

CHAPTER 7: STEPS TO PROTECT YOUR INNOVATIONS AND INVENTIONS

Conduct a patent search: Before investing resources into your ideas or a product, make sure to conduct a patent search to ensure that the idea is not already patented by someone else.

Develop a minimum viable product (MVP): Start with a basic version of the product or service that can be tested on the market. This will help you validate the idea and identify any potential issues early on.

Build a brand: Develop a unique brand that resonates with your target market. This includes creating a logo, tagline, and visual identity that communicate your company's values.

Focus on user experience: Make sure the product or service from your ideas is user-friendly and provides an exceptional experience for customers. This can be achieved through user testing and feedback.

Leverage social media: Use social media to connect

with potential customers and build brand awareness. Platforms such as Facebook, Instagram, and LinkedIn can be powerful marketing tools.

Create a referral program: Encourage existing customers to refer new customers by offering incentives or rewards. Word-of-mouth marketing can be a powerful marketing tool.

Continuously innovate: Keep the product or service fresh by continuously adding new features or improving existing ones. This will help you stay ahead of the competition.

Seek out mentors and advisors: Find experienced mentors and advisors who can provide guidance and support as you build your company.

Monitor key metrics: Monitor key metrics such as customer acquisition cost, lifetime value of a customer, and churn rate. This will help you make informed decisions and pivot if necessary.

Establish a strong company culture: Create a company culture that values innovation, collaboration, and diversity. This will help you attract and retain top talent and create a positive work environment.

CHAPTER 8: SUSTAINABILITY OF THE IDEAS YOU WANT TO USE TO MAKE MILLIONS

Attend industry conferences and events: Attend conferences and events to network with other industry professionals and learn about the latest trends and technologies.

Build a community: Create a community of customers, advocates, and industry influencers around your product or service. This can be achieved through social media, forums, or online communities.

Establish strategic partnerships: Identify potential partners who can help you expand your reach or add value to your product or service. This could include suppliers, distributors, or complementary businesses.

Develop a strong online presence: Create a website that showcases your product or service and provides easy access to information and support. Use search engine optimization (SEO) techniques to improve your website's visibility in search results.

Conduct regular market research: Continuously gather feedback from customers and conduct market research to stay on top of industry trends and customer needs.

Hire the right people: Build a team of talented and dedicated individuals who share your vision and values. Look for people who bring diverse perspectives and skills to the table.

Develop a long-term vision: Create a long-term vision for the company and set ambitious but achievable goals. This will help keep everyone aligned and focused on the big picture.

Secure intellectual property rights: Protect your intellectual property by obtaining patents, trademarks, or copyrights where applicable. This will prevent others from copying your product or service.

Monitor your competition: Keep an eye on your competition and identify areas where you can differentiate yourself or improve your product or service.

Measure and optimize: Measure key performance indicators (KPIs) and optimize your product or service based on the data. This will help you make informed decisions and improve your business.

CHAPTER 9: PATH TO A LIFESTYLE OF SUCCESS WHILE YOU WAIT FOR IDEAS

Here are some steps to help you fund your project when the idea comes.

Maintain a comfortable lifestyle: Teachers who are financially stable can afford to turn their ideas into money.

Invest in your professional development: By investing in yourself by attending conferences, taking courses, and participating in other professional development opportunities. This can improve your reasoning skills and open doors to ideas.

Save for your project: Save some money for your future project. Setting aside a portion of your income each month to implement your ideas when they come helps you avoid borrowing from people who do not believe in your ideas.

Set a budget: Create a budget that outlines your income and expenses, and stick to it. This will help you manage your money and avoid overspending.

Live below your means: Try to live below your means and avoid unnecessary expenses. Consider cutting back on eating out, entertainment, and other non-essential expenses.

Consider additional income streams: Consider taking on additional part-time work or starting a side business to supplement your income. This will help you invest in big ideas that can change your life for the better.

Seek financial advice: Consider meeting with a financial advisor or taking a personal finance course to learn more about managing your money and building wealth.

Overall, transforming your ideas into a million-dollar company requires discipline, smart financial planning, and commitment to long-term financial goals. By managing your money wisely, you can achieve your dream and enjoy a secure future.

CHAPTER 10: CONCLUSION WITH ADVICE

As I conclude, it is essential to recognize and honor the treasure that teachers truly are. To this end, here are some key pieces of advice: "The Treasure That Teachers Trade Away to Make Others Millionaires, Yet They Remain Poor" calls on readers to recognize and identify these immeasurable ideas teachers trade away every time to make others millionaires and use them to transform their lives to become millionaire teachers. I have shown in this book that teachers make others millionaires through their ideas during lessons. The way to uplift your standards and build a brighter future for yourself is by valuing your ideas and having an entrepreneurial mindset. Your ideas are worth millions! Here is advice for teachers:

Engage in self-reflection: Teachers should engage in self-reflection over their lives and should use all methods presented in this book to become a better and valued person in society.

Never lose sight of the value of your work: Teachers should always remember that their ideas have immeasurable value in changing their own future and status. Despite the challenges, they should continue to be proud of their profession and the difference they make in others' lives.

Advocate for change: Teachers, along with their allies, must continue to advocate for policy changes and systemic reforms that address the issues they face, including fair and competitive salaries, adequate resources, and recognition of their work.

Prioritize well-being: Teachers should prioritize their physical, mental, and emotional well-being. Self-care is crucial to maintain a healthy work-life balance and prevent burnout.

Engage in community-driven approaches: Teachers should explore and advocate for community-driven approaches to education that prioritize students' well-being and promote equity, diversity, and inclusivity in the classroom.

Engage in ongoing learning: Teachers should be lifelong learners themselves, staying curious, open-minded, and adaptable to changes in education and students' needs.

Build supportive networks: Teachers should build support networks with fellow teachers, administrators, and other stakeholders in education to share ideas, resources, and support.

Seek professional development: Continuous professional development is vital for teachers to stay updated with best practices and effectively meet their students' needs. Teachers should seek high-quality professional development opportunities.

Embrace teacher leadership: Teachers should embrace

leadership opportunities within their schools, communities, and the education system. Their voices and expertise are invaluable in shaping education policy and practice.

See you at the top.

ACKNOWLEDGEMENT

"The Treasure That Teachers Trade Away To Make Others Millionaires, Yet They Remain Poor" is a thought-provoking book that delves into the often-overlooked challenges and sacrifices teachers face in their noble profession. In this book, readers will gain a deeper understanding of teachers' remarkable dedication and passion. They will also learn how they inspired others to become millionaires but remain poor.

In today's fast-paced world, where monetary gains often define success, it is crucial to let teachers know that the trainer can also become rich even while facing numerous obstacles to shaping young minds and nurturing a love of learning. Throughout this book, we hope to honor their tireless efforts and raise awareness of the treasure they trade away to make others millionaires.

One of the key themes explored in this book is the systemic issues that plague the teaching profession. Teachers are frequently confronted with low pay, which fails to reflect their immense value to society. Moreover, inadequate resources and lack of support further compound classroom challenges. By highlighting these issues, readers will appreciate teachers' resilience and determination.

Through powerful narratives and real-life anecdotes, "The Treasure That Teachers Trade Away To Make Others Millionaires, Yet They Remain Poor" serves as a wake-up call for teachers.

As you embark on this enlightening journey through this book, be prepared to transform your perspective on the teaching profession. The stories shared in some chapters will inspire you to become an advocate for change, even as a teacher.

It is my hope that this book will serve as a testament to teachers' unwavering spirit, begin to inspire you with newfound hope as it shows you what a treasure teachers are to society, and guide you towards a future in which educators are fully recognized and valued.

ABOUT THE AUTHOR

Maxwell Steindacruz

The author of "The Treasure That Teachers Trade Away To Make Others Millionaires, Yet They Remain Poor" is an experienced educator, a passionate advocate for teachers' rights, and an ardent believer in education's transformative power. With a deep understanding of the challenges and realities faced by teachers in today's society, the author brings an unusual perspective to the table.   The author explores the variety of ways teachers' effort and actions enrich others while they themselves struggle to make ends meet. He has delved into the systemic issues that affect educators' financial stability, professional growth, and work-life balance, making a compelling case for reform and an appreciation for the teaching community. Through this eye-opening book, the author sheds light on the often overlooked aspects that teachers use to enrich others and explains how teachers can use the same secret to become millionaires.

www.ingramcontent.com/pod-product-compliance
Lightning Source LLC
Chambersburg PA
CBHW071006260726
48661CB00007B/2819